The Fear of Love and Loss

and Loss

Niomi Sterling

BookLeaf Publishing

The Fear of Love and Loss © 2022 Niomi Sterling

All rights reserved.

Niomi Sterling asserts the moral right to be identified as author of this work.

Presentation by *BookLeaf Publishing*

Web: www.bookleafpub.com

E-mail: info@bookleafpub.com

ISBN: 9789357619769

First edition 2022

Dedicated to my beautiful grandmother, Faith Bailey.

You are the prototype, the seed that bore fruit.

A that gift has never been bound by time.

Your GOD

What do you make of your God?
He and I ain't been speaking

I used to think Jesus was the hero
But lately that dude been tweakin' like...
How you gonna keep doing me like this bro?

I know you did the cross for our sins and
I know we all still sinnin' but..

...Our hearts weren't built for this type of loss.

And people keep talking to me about endings
As if everything in life is some sort of fairytale
But I'm tired of listening to you talk about
endings as if they are a choice to engage with

As if I'm not crying myself to sleep at night just
to get some respite..
from the anger
and the quiet

and the loud, loud voices telling me she's not
here!

She's not here, and it's your fault!
It was YOUR GOD that taught me how to lose
Turned me sacrilege
taught me the meaning of the true L

It looks like numbing out just to make it to the next day

Fist balling
Street fights that take the place of real tears

It was YOUR GOD who said I was strong enough
Man enough
Faith enough to move mountains
and then clawed the faith right from under my skin

It was YOUR GOD that made me a believer in a hell on earth
Because of him I don't know how to pray
without seeing her face anymore...

And reminding myself that theres not returning from the far away place.

I begged her to stay...

But it was Your God who stole her anyway.

I love God, I swear

I want to talk to God again...
I know we ain't speaking,
but I'm finding it hard again

I'm fighting the fear again
I'm losing the peace of me...

I'm losing the grace in me
The walls are closing in and screaming for Faith

I want to talk to God again
ask him why he's given me this load to lift

What is my story?
Where does my worry rest its head?

I love God, I swear
But we ain't been speakin'

I love God, I swear
but it's my grandmother's doing

I love God, I swear
but he took her from me

I love God, I swear
I love God, I swear
I love God, I swear

But for now...
I can't seem to find the words to stay.

Some days I wonder...

Some days I wonder if you ever loved me at all
Not because you didn't show it
But because how could you?

Maybe you didn't know me
Maybe you wanted to, but we were too far apart
Maybe cognition was our great divider and I
wonder if love can live there?

In the black box of us

I tried to love you
Maybe you tried too

Maybe you tried beyond the fog
Maybe there was always a little glimmer
Where I broke through and...

You became the best of you

Sometimes I wonder if you ever loved me at all
Sometimes I wonder you wanted to, but couldn't

...

Sometimes I wonder if in the end
You couldn't love anyone
Sometimes I wonder, if you were just like me

Asking about You

My phone still brings up memories of you
and I wonder if its trying to bait me into
calling...
Into memory lane of what we once were

My phone asks if I like the new collage?
It's the third wheel of our love affair

It asks me questions as if it disapproves of our
goodbye
My phone keeps wondering about you
It asks if you're doing okay out there in big, bad
world

It wonders if you ate
If you slept well
If you took your medication
If you need me there

It wonders if I broke you
It wonder if I didn't do it right

It wonders if goodbyes will ever feel the way I
want them to...

Like an agreement.
Like a purposeful end.

Like two people acknowledging that not all
beautiful things can be kept
Like maybe we run free of each other but not
away

Because of the love...

And the well wishes...

And the pictures in our phones
popping up year after year
asking about you

Passing

It's the way things pass as if they were never
here
As if there was never this cavity in my chest
filled with the misgivings of another

It's the way people call each other seasonal
Like we all come back around one day
Like we'll wake up one day and stare into each
others eyes with the same hope of yesterday

As if that will be the thing that saves us
This endless loop of living

But when we leave, they'll call it passing
As if we never intended to stay.

How Important Could it Be?

It's important what we do here
How we say goodbye
It's important how we look into each other's eyes

It's important to see the heart hurting
It's important to grieve it
release it

It's important what we do here
engaging in the wishing
Wishing it were not the last

... maybe the first
...maybe the worst

It's important that we be here
What is in an end, if not a new beginning

It's important that we stand here
knowing
unknowing
and knowing again

That moments cannot be moved
Moments cannot be captured

moments are undoubtedly fleeting
and time is a friend to no man.

I want to feel more ...

I think what I'm struggling with ...
is trying to capture the feeling of feeling

I'm a disassociating heroine
I'm in the ring and can't feel the punches

Be brave they say
but brave to me and you are different things

For you brave is power, a martyr, a king
For me brave is flower, a widow, a stream

So flip it on its head I said
Let's change everything
Bravery is vulnerable
Feel everything

Grief #8

Grief feel like being low-key drunk,
floating in the sea of your ancestors

Arms open wide screaming in silence,
come find me.

Grief feels like letting the sun warm your face,
while the sound of your own breath clouds your
judgement.

When two hands grab either side, they'll
whisper,
come with me.

You will recognize their broken English
You will laugh and smile
Three girls unafraid of the unknown.

Bendicion, you'll hear
I love you
Come with me

Who says what? you won't know
Bur grief feels like not knowing.

While the ocean waves crash into you, on the
Caribbean sea.

Grief reminds that sometimes it takes 2 bottles
of tequila
and swimming carefree like at the pool behind
abuela's house
to feel free

... or alive
... or something

I love you
Bendicion
Come with me

You'll reply
Back... in broken english
Loud enough so even the angels can't help but
agree.

Magician's Tale

I wish I could say I learned how to say "i love
you" in different languages
...in different tongues

Instead I've received it in accented English
Begging for me to understand that in this
country, you love me
It wasn't your fault
I should have warned you

It will happen time and again,
An insufferable magic trick
Those three words mean nothing coming from
you
Coming from any of the five boroughs or 50
states

None of the continents or seven seas
you don't love me, you want to love me.

This is the magic: I've no idea why you're here,
how you got here.

Maybe it's a punishment
I should blame my parents for making me look
lovable across oceans
Across hurricanes
Across subway lines and commutes as long as
this lifeline

What a tragedy

Across buying cars
Across marriages and relationships
You love me in spite of... it all

You love me you say,
In accented English.

Why not say it native?
Maybe then it will mean more
Maybe then it will reveal its deceit to you
Maybe then I won't have to stand in front of you
eyes sullen
heart open
Again.
You don't.

Like moon and sun
you want to love me
But at the end of the day,
you won't.

My love.

Grieving you came like a hurricane
The ones that ravaged the house in Puerto Rico

When I noticed you were truly gone, it came on
the day of the parade
All the flags waved in the air and I could
suddenly smell the sea
I could suddenly sense the streams of the lakes
we played in
The waves suddenly washed over me, bringing
with them your scent

The way you smiled in the kitchen
The way you hummed in the streets

Dear abuelita,
It was always you for me

Heavy water drops on a tin roof
pounding like the maracas your son used to play
pounding at the nape of my neck, you're gone
so why did you choose today?

To creep out from my memory
To seep deep into my coffee coated dreams
To play your tricks on me in a language I never
knew

Abuelita,
I was today years old when I missed you
You held away the pain

But now it hits me with brute force
blasting away bridges
roofs and cars
blasting away the carefully built cottages that
protected my heart

Abuelita,
today I know you're gone
but the flags still go down the road in Times
Square
masking as if they were on the streets of Caguas

I imagine them shouting in your honor
All hail the Queen or Boriquen
Lydia, my love,
this hurricane can only be in your name.

My Mother

My mother
God Bless her
Loves turkey and cheese

I imagine she was born in a bread manger
engulfed in wafting winds of wheat and rye

This element would never leave her
The desire to be held, soft and warm

She would brew it into her coffee on Sunday
mornings
and relax into the dream of all she couldn't be

On this day, My mother
God Bless her
knows that she has given away all that she has
ever loved

She had sewn it into her daughters, her partners
Nurtured, watered, and grew them to leave
Never fully reciprocating her offering
My mother
God Bless her
This is all she knew

Tomorrow, my father says,
buy her a 1/2 pound of turkey and a 1/4 pound of
cheese
Why? I ask
No response.

My why builds until it boils
becomes peppered with her smile
the scent of her bread
the warmth of her embrace
the bend of the corner of the page of her favorite
book
patiently waiting her next chapter

The story untold, less written
In this story everything she touches turns to gold
There is only love
there is only liberation
there is only trust
there is only peace

And by the end of course
there's turkey and cheese

God Bless her
My mother
Born in a bread manger
baked by the sun

Down & Out

I've been down so long it looks like up to me
heart torn
I've been down so long I forget to breathe
heart worn
I've been down so long I can't see clearly
perfect storm

When I left you it wasn't because I wanted out
I wanted in
I wanted in so deep that I could swim
away from the pain

I wanted your love to comfort me
I wanted it to be my life raft
To hold on to you when it got too much
and it felt too far
and everything started crashing

I never wanted out I wanted in from the storm
I wanted a safe place to stand
I wanted what love looked like
Before the warning signs
Before the, "don't run"
Before the Slippery when wet...

I wanted joy, deep joy
to know the choice was right
I wanted in
In the middle of the night
when the meal was cooked right
and the drinks were fresh
and the TV was waiting on our glazed over eyes
and laughs

I never wanted out, I wanted in
To give it on more shot
but when the rubble and debris fell at our feet
You had already changed the lock.

I want to write you love poems

I want to write love poems but I can't seem to
find them
buried under all this life I live
Love poems about the sun and the moon
the sand and the sea
escape me

Now the poems are about the next day above
ground
and the next, and the next
and how supremely valuable time is when you
are given the space to acknowledge it

Flow through it
Claim it in the name of your patron saint
Is it too late to write you love poems?
And if I don't...
How long will you stay?

What would it be like to be in a serious relationship

People say serious, so seriously
And then I thought of you
You who existed before the very serious me
So comfortable
So uninhibited
So fractured
& together, so whole
I can't help but text you on the days I feel lost

You, still a place that feels like home
You, still an open door for me
Even as I have shape-shifted
Flown away
Called by other names
Become so... strange

When I think of love
It is still the smell of your t-shirt that reminds
me of possibility
You call me the yellow daffodil
Beauty and the bee
Where there is you, there will always be honey

So serious, and sweet.

Idc.

And I don't care whose loving you today...
I'm loving you through all of your tomorrows.

The Eulogy

So here is the day I thought would never come
Experiencing the finite nature of life is one of
the most devastating things I've had the
displeasure of knowing

And yet it seems that in life we live through
many deaths
some external and very many more internal
Often those give life to something else,
something beautiful, and I try to remember that
every time this get hard.

But on that note, this is the second death... not
the first.
The first truly broke me
The first was losing touch in the metaphorical
sense of the word

My first best friend was so deeply loved by me
We had bubble baths, and blankies and we had
pets and songs
We had remedies and lunches

We had moments where she saved me
... and I had hoped to do the same

I remember thinking, this is one of the best
people I know and even though my world was so
small
I'm convinced that remained true over years of
growing and learning.

Never hearing my name from her lips
Never singing any more songs
Never having any more tight hugs
...well that was the biggest loss for me

But this one is the physical
Which I did my best to love equally
even when she didn't seem the same
even when she seemed she was no longer mine

I had to let her go, in order to love the new
person that stood in her wake
so incredibly different
but I loved her

And there were new laughs
and new moments
and new meanings

So today I mourn that loss
Which somehow mends something in me.

It's as if I'd held half a broken heart for years
and the other half has come home to complete it

So now I can see the whole
and remember, and love, and grieve in fullness
without cursing that first loss

That whole heart now beats
and that's a funny thing to say at this time

It's whole now and the full picture of my best
friend,
all thirty years that I got to know her
is finally there
Smiling back at me in the familiar way I knew
she would

And now I can say I love you, and it can mean, I
loved you
At 5
At 10
At 20
and at 30

And I will love you still
and keep you safe in the arms of the lord
May you rest your weary head on the angel
wings he has set forth for you
We will love you still, forever more.

Although it hurts

I am quite happy to say that I have been brave
Been afraid and done it anyway
Knew the consequences and took the risk

And although I am a little bruised,
a bit worn and perhaps forever longing

I'm happy to say that I let my heart choose love
for a change
And even in the aftermath, only grown better for
it.

The desert

The desert will teach you how to survive
the moments you never thought you could

Printed in the USA
CPSIA information can be obtained
at www.ICGtesting.com
LVHW011540050124
767941LV00091B/5146